What's Inside Your Tummy, Mommy?

Abby Cocovini

For Rich, Ramona,
and Samson,
with love

—A. C.

Henry Holt and Company, LLC
PUBLISHERS SINCE 1866
175 Fifth Avenue
New York, New York 10010
www.HenryHoltKids.com

Henry Holt® is a registered trademark of Henry Holt and Company, LLC.
Copyright © 2007 by Abby Cocovini
All rights reserved.
Distributed in Canada by H. B. Fenn and Company Ltd.
First published in the United States in 2008 by Henry Holt and Company, LLC.
Originally published in England in a slightly different form in 2007 by
Random House Children's Books, a division of the Random House Group Ltd,
London, Sydney, Auckland, Johannesburg, New Delhi,
and agencies throughout the world.

Library of Congress Control Number: 2007930591

ISBN-13: 978-0-8050-8760-4
ISBN-10: 0-8050-8760-5

First American Edition—2008
Printed in China on acid-free paper. ∞

1 3 5 7 9 10 8 6 4 2

The images in this book offer only a
rough guide. Actual size will vary depending
on the baby and its mommy.

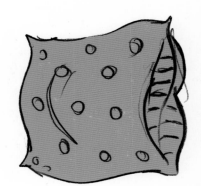

Inside a mommy's tummy is a special place called her womb. Part of the womb is filled with liquid, a bit like a warm, squishy cushion.

This is where a baby will grow. It will stay there for nine months, growing and changing shape until it is ready to be born.

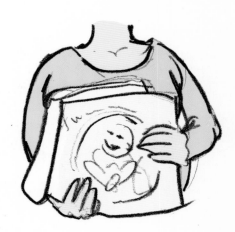

Turn the pages of this book to find out what happens in a mommy's tummy. And if the mommy holds the book up to her belly, you will see what the baby looks like (actual size) inside her every month!

Just think . . . you used to look like that!

Count the baby's age in days and weeks using the calendar strip at the bottom of each page.

Week Fourteen						
92	93	94	95	96	97	98

Month 1
Weeks 1 to 4

At first the baby is so teeny-tiny, you can't even see it! It doesn't look like a baby yet.

Just a little circle of jelly.

It sticks to the side of the mommy's womb and then it starts to gROW.

The baby is so small that it has a special name. It's called an embryo.

The baby grows very quickly. It doubles in size every day for the first four weeks.

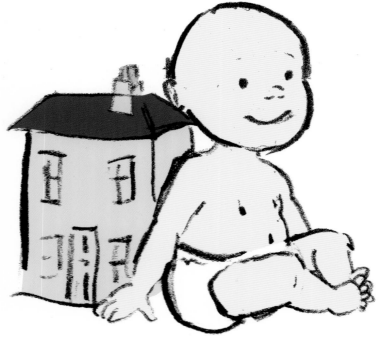

If it did that for nine months, it would be bigger than a house!

The baby is smaller than a grain of rice.

Week One							Week Two				
1	2	3	4	5	6	7	8	9	10	11	12	13	14

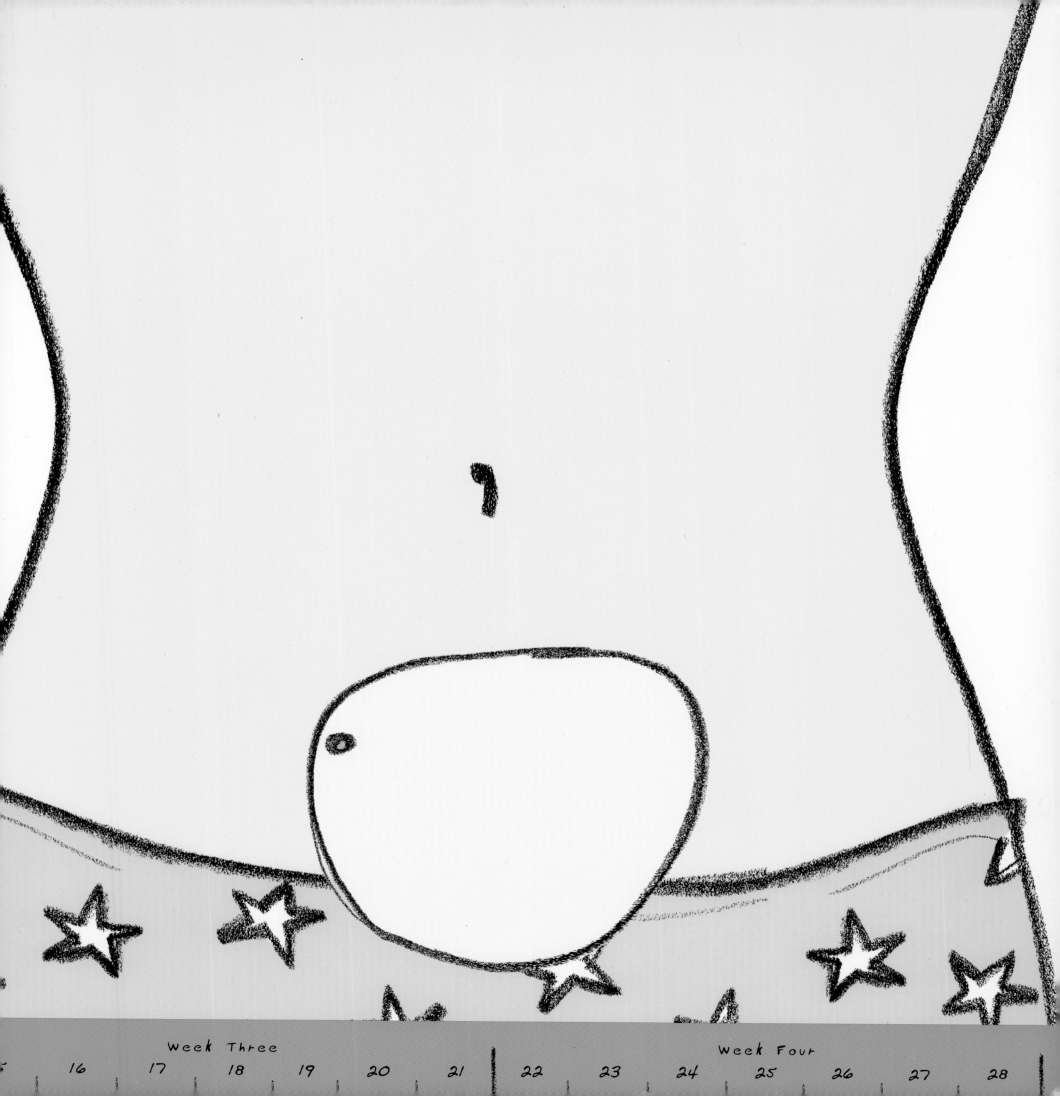

Month 2
Weeks 5 to 9

The baby has grown and changed shape.
It has a big head and a body. But it also has a tail.
It looks a bit like a tadpole!

Don't worry—the tail will go away soon!

The baby has little bumps on its body,
which are growing into arms and legs.

It can already turn its head and stretch.

A tube connects the
developing baby to its mommy.

This is the umbilical cord.

It is very important because
it brings food and oxygen from
the mommy to the baby and
takes wastes away.

*The baby is
as big as a
baked bean.*

Month 3
Weeks 10 to 13

The baby is as big as an orange.

Now the baby is starting to look more like a baby.

It has lost its tail. It has fingers and toes. It even has fingernails that are as tiny as grains of sand!

There is a lot of space in the womb for the baby to move. It can kick and wriggle around.

But it is still so small, the mommy won't even feel it.

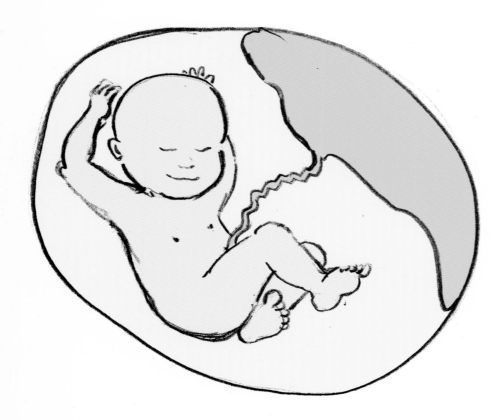

The baby can open and close its mouth and put its hand on its head.

The baby is now as long as a grown-up's finger.

6 Months to Go! That's spring & summer.

Month 4
Weeks 14 to 18

The baby pees 15 times a day!

The baby is getting fatter and its hair is growing.

Crunch, crunch, crunch

It's starting to hear! But only things from inside its mommy, like . . .

her heart thumping . . .

her blood flowing . . .

and her food being swallowed.

It can point its feet, close its hand, and even suck its thumb.

da-dum, da-dum, da-dum

The baby's also good at making faces!

The baby is as big as a medium-sized melon.

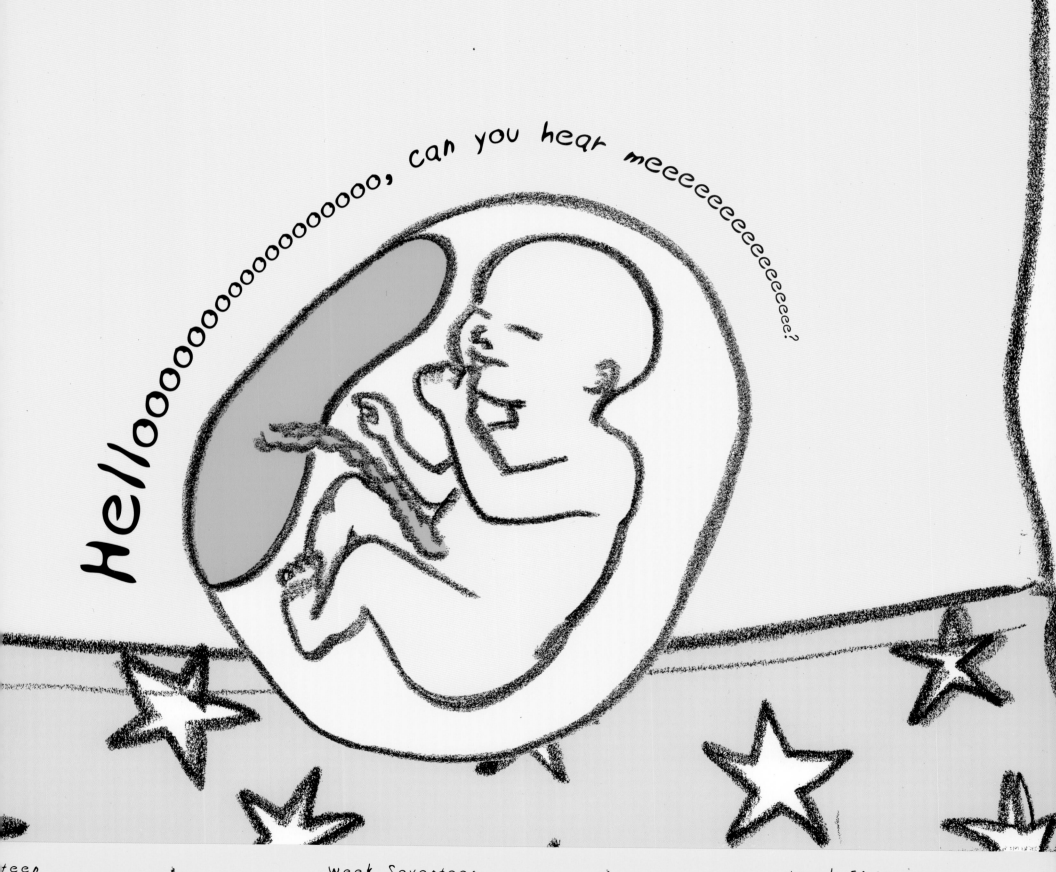

The baby is as big as a carton of milk.

Month 5
Weeks 19 to 22

**Now the mommy can feel the baby move.
And if you're lucky, so can you!**

The baby might move when the
mommy rubs her tummy . . .

. . . aaaaaaaaahhhhhhhhh!

or when the baby hears music . . .

or its mommy's voice.

La la la, my special baby

All sorts of things are starting to happen.
Soft, fine hair has grown all over the baby's body.
And now a waterproof coating
covers the baby's skin to keep it
clean and protected.

**The baby
can move its eyes
from side to side.
But it still can't
open them.**

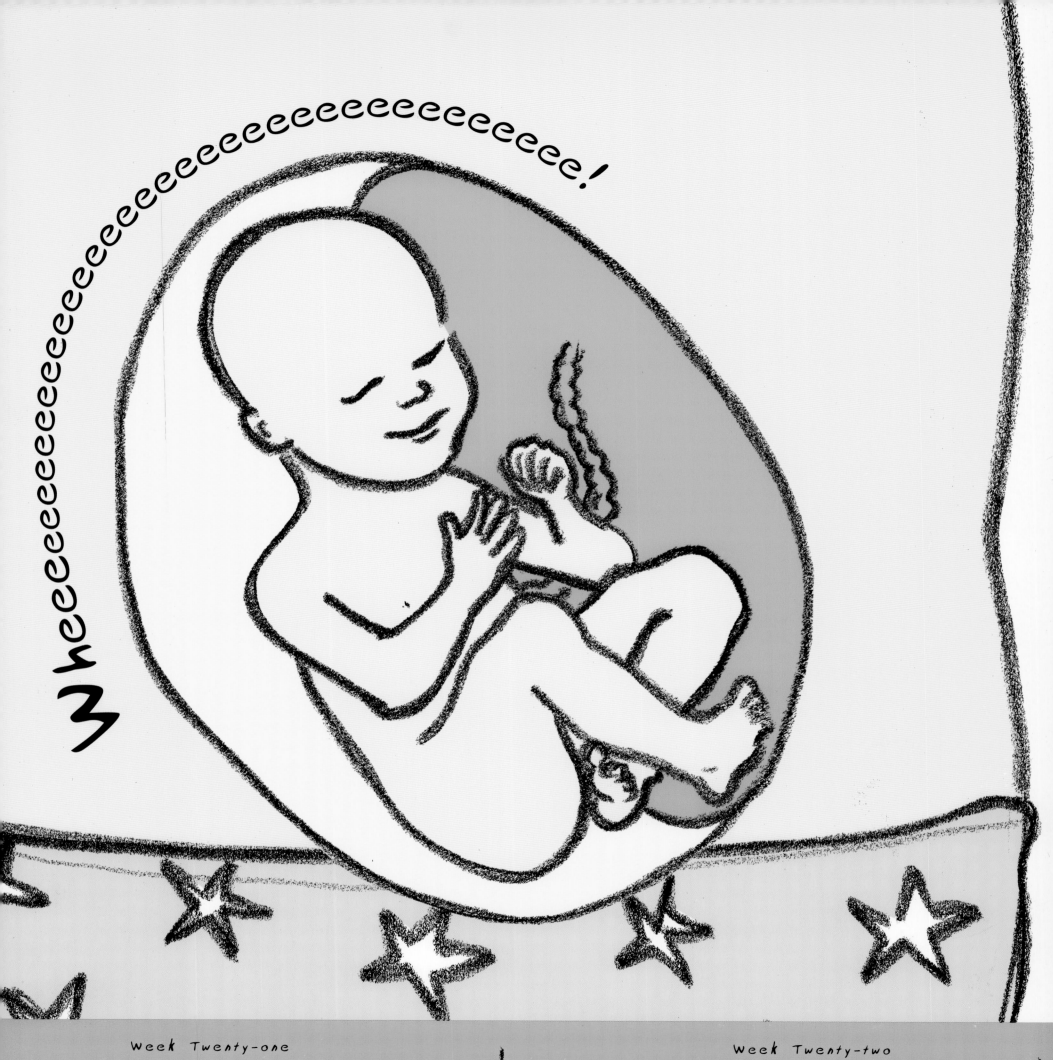

The baby is as big as a large pineapple.

Month 6
Weeks 23 to 26

The baby's getting bigger!

And there's not much space to move around. So you might see the baby moving in the mommy's tummy!

The baby is sleeping a lot.
And it could be dreaming!

It often goes to sleep when its mommy walks around, because the walking rocks it back and forth.

Now the baby can open its eyes!

And it might even turn its head if you shine a light at the mommy's tummy.

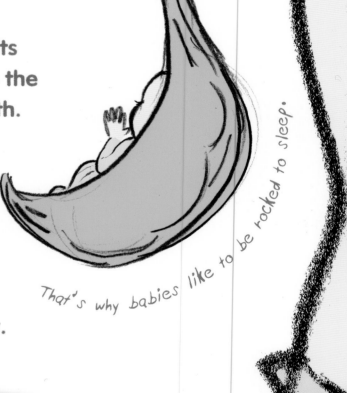

That's why babies like to be rocked to sleep.

If you put your ear to the mommy's belly, you might hear the baby's heartbeat.

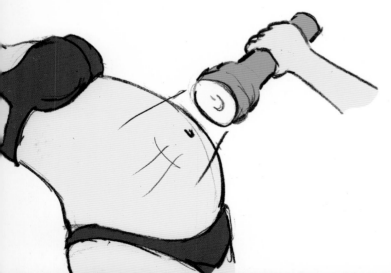

Month 7
Weeks 27 to 31

The baby is getting bigger and fatter!

The baby can blink its eyes now.

Its weight can double this month. That's like a ten-year-old boy turning into a man in just four weeks.

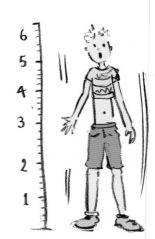

The baby knows its mommy's voice. And it might remember songs or sounds that it hears a lot.

Twinkle, twinkle, little star...

How I wonder what you are...

Most of the time the baby just sleeps. It wakes up for only two hours a day.
That's like waking up only for lunch and dinner!

The baby is as big as a loaf of bread.

BREAD

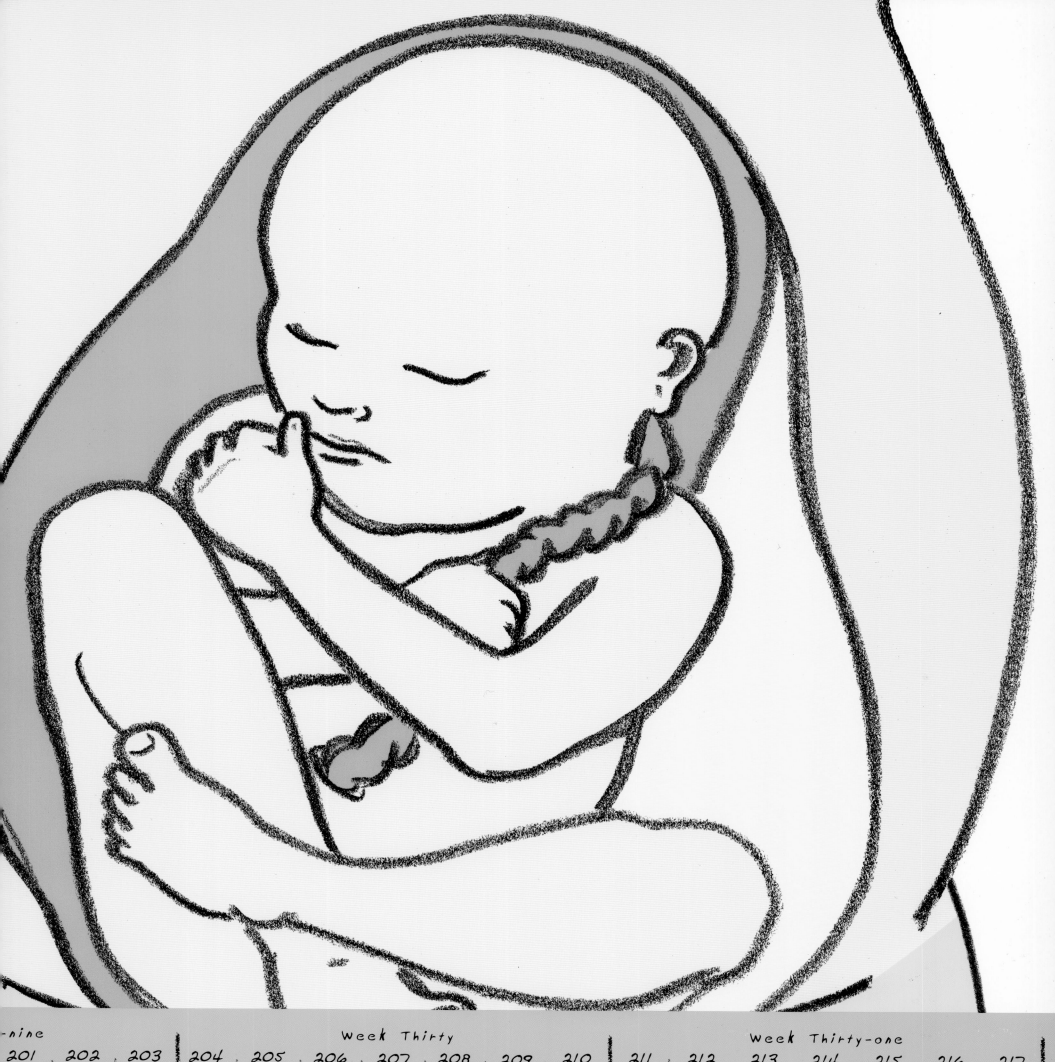

Month 8
Weeks 32 to 36

The baby is **bigger** than ever!

The baby is almost as big as a pumpkin.

Its fingernails have grown so long that it can even scratch itself.

The baby can do so many things—

listening . . .

blinking . . .

kicking . . .

sucking its thumb.

The baby stays upside down now so there's more room for its head, and so it is ready to come out of the mommy head-first.

And now it's doing all these things as much as it can, sometimes for nearly half an hour at a time. *Phew!*

stretching . . .

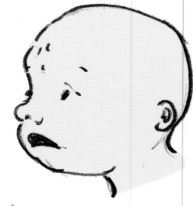

frowning . . .

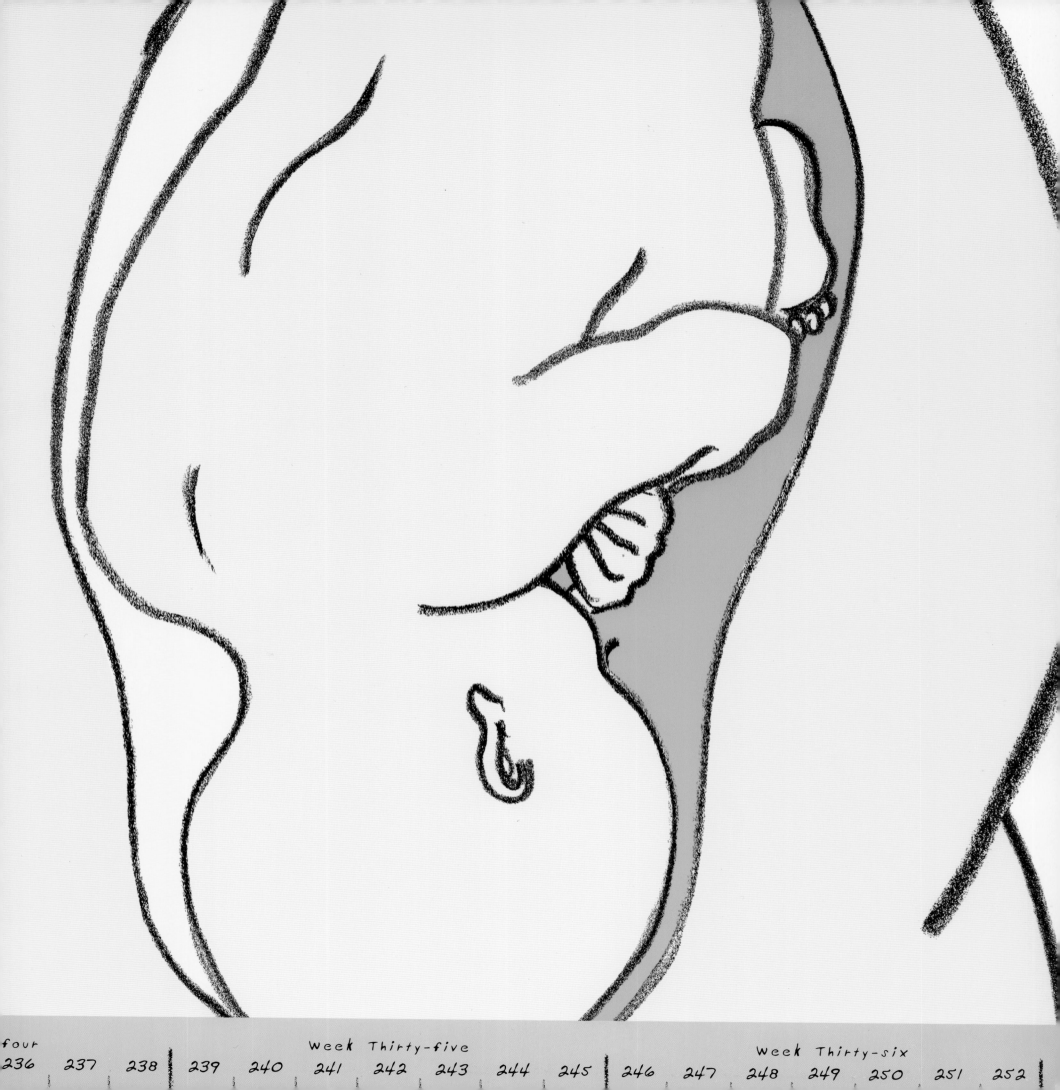

Month 9
Weeks 37 to 40

Now the baby is ready to come out!

It is so big that there is hardly any room to move around.
But it's still listening and blinking and frowning.

The baby is getting ready for its birthday.

The hair and waterproof coating on the baby's body are falling off.

When the time is right, the mommy starts to squeeze the baby out.

It's a lot of hard work.

At last the baby comes out.

Hip, hip, hooray!

Welcome Home!

It's as big as . . . **a baby!**